First Facts™

Community Helpers at Work

A Day in the Life of an
Emergency Medical
Technician

by Heather Adamson

Consultant:
Rob Farmer, EMT-P
Firefighter/Paramedic
City of Upper Arlington, Ohio, Fire Division

Capstone
press

Mankato, Minnesota

First Facts is published by Capstone Press
151 Good Counsel Drive, P.O. Box 669, Mankato, Minnesota 56002
http://www.capstonepress.com

Library of Congress Cataloging-in-Publication Data
Adamson, Heather, 1974–
    A day in the life of an Emergency Medical Technician / by Heather Adamson.
    p. cm.— (First facts. Community helpers at work)
    Includes bibliographical references and index.
    Contents: How do emergency medical technicians start their shifts?—Do EMTs work alone?
What do EMTs wear?—What do EMTs do when they are not helping patients?—What kind of
skills do EMTs need?—What tools do EMTs use?—How do patients get to the hospital?—What
happens at the end of a shift?—Amazing but true!
    ISBN 0-7368-2507-X (hardcover)
    1. Emergency medical technicians—Juvenile literature. [1. Emergency medical technicians.
2. Emergency medical services. 3. Occupations.] I. Title. II. Series.
RA645.5.A23 2004
616.02'5'023—dc22   2003015023

Credits
Jennifer Bergstrom, series designer; Enoch Peterson, book designer; Gary Sundermeyer,
    photographer; Eric Kudalis, product planning editor

Photo Credits
All photographs Capstone Press/Gary Sundermeyer, except p. 20, Corbis/Bettmann

Artistic effects
Comstock

Capstone Press thanks Eugene Taylor and Rural/Metro Ambulance of Sioux Falls, South Dakota,
    for their assistance in the photographing of this book.
Capstone Press also thanks David Boer and Amy Marsh of South Dakota Emergency Medical
    Services for Children for their assistance in creating this book.

1 2 3 4 5 6 09 08 07 06 05 04

Table of Contents

How do emergency medical technicians start their shifts?

Emergency medical **technicians** (EMTs) report to their stations to start their **shifts**. Eugene starts his shift at 7:00 in the morning. He checks the equipment on the **ambulance**. He makes sure everything is ready to use.

 Fun Fact:
In 2000, about 172,000 people worked as EMTs in the United States.

Do EMTs work alone?

EMTs always work in teams. Eugene and Stacy work together. They lift the patient into the ambulance.

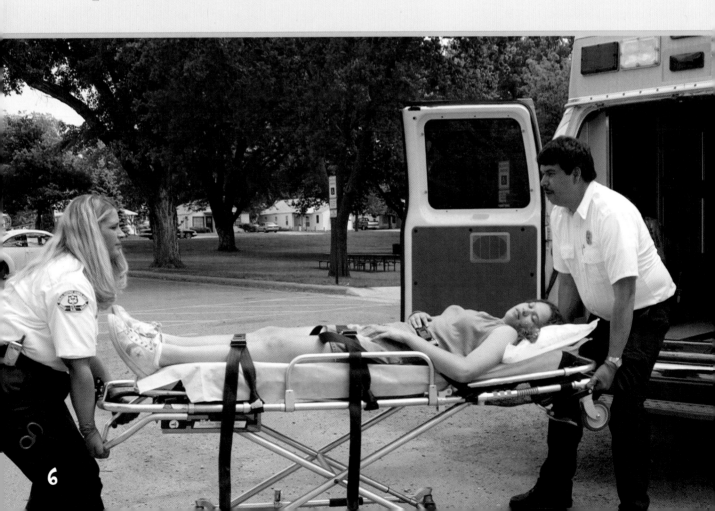

9:30 in the morning

Dispatchers, police officers, and firefighters also help EMTs. In an **emergency**, they work together to keep people safe and treat people who are hurt.

What do EMTs wear?

EMTs wear uniforms to show they that are emergency workers. Their pants have many pockets to hold supplies. Eugene wears gloves to treat a cut. Gloves help stop the spread of **germs**.

11:30 in the morning

What do EMTs do when they are not helping patients?

EMTs do many things when they are not treating patients. They learn about new equipment. Sometimes they rest and eat at the station. Today, Eugene and Stacy teach children how to ride bikes and play safely.

What kind of skills do EMTs need?

EMTs use math, reading, writing, and other skills every day. Eugene uses a small computer to measure a patient's blood sugar. Stacy reads the **pulse**. They record the **data**.

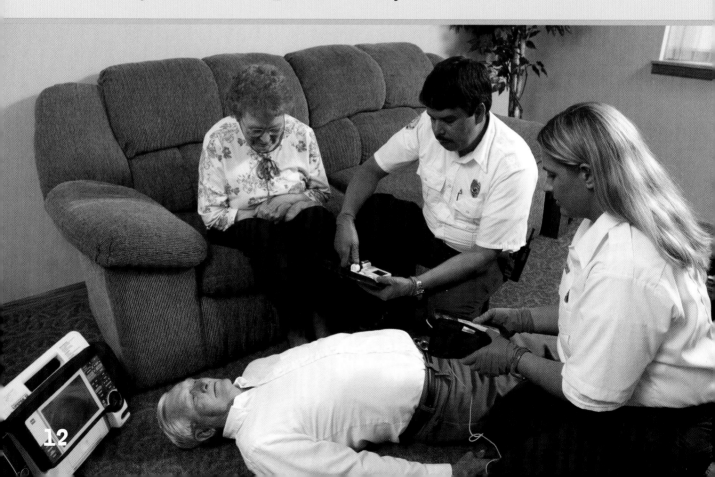

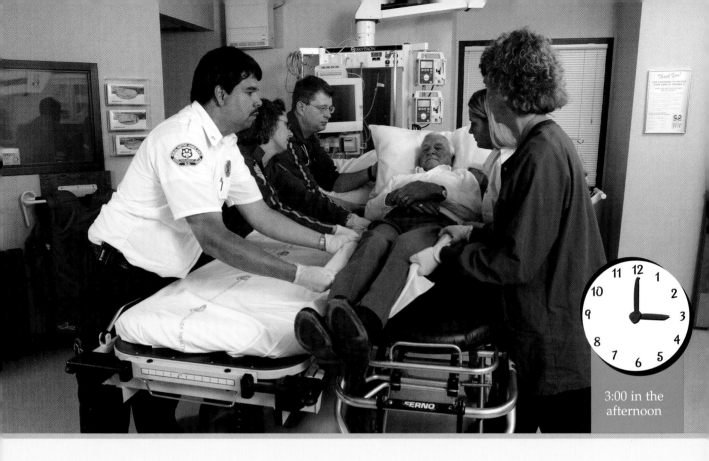

3:00 in the
afternoon

At the hospital, Eugene and Stacy
tell the nurse about the patient. After
the nurse takes over, they write a report
to put in the patient's **chart**.

What tools do EMTs use?

EMTs use many tools. Bandages cover cuts and scrapes. Splints hold bones in place. Eugene puts a collar around the patient's neck. Then, he straps her on a backboard. It keeps her spine safe. Stacy squeezes air from a bag into the patient's lungs to help her breathe.

4:30 in the afternoon

14

 Fun Fact:
The spinal column is made up of 33 bones called vertebrae.

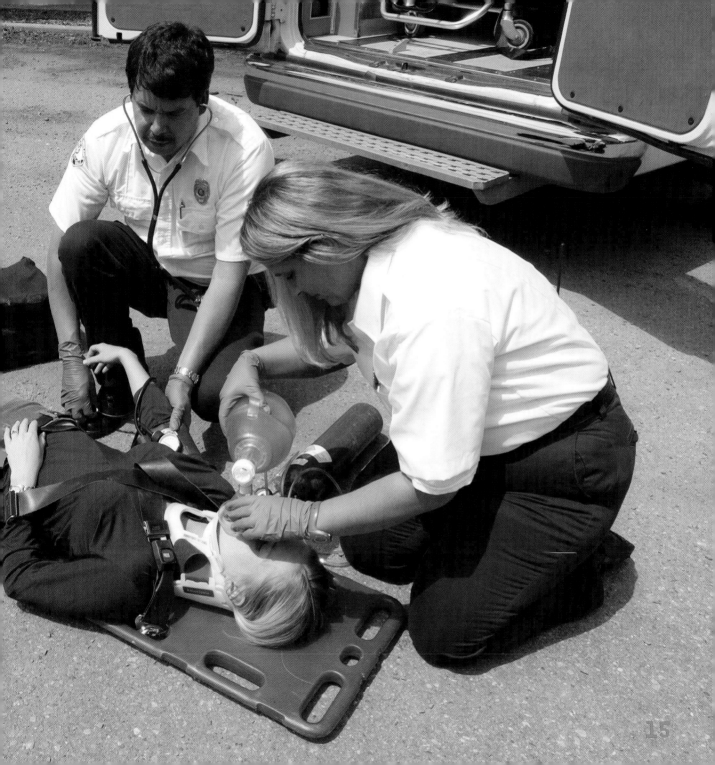

How do patients get to the hospital?

EMTs usually use ambulances to take patients to the hospital. The flashing lights and sirens warn cars to pull over. Stacy drives while Eugene cares for the patient.

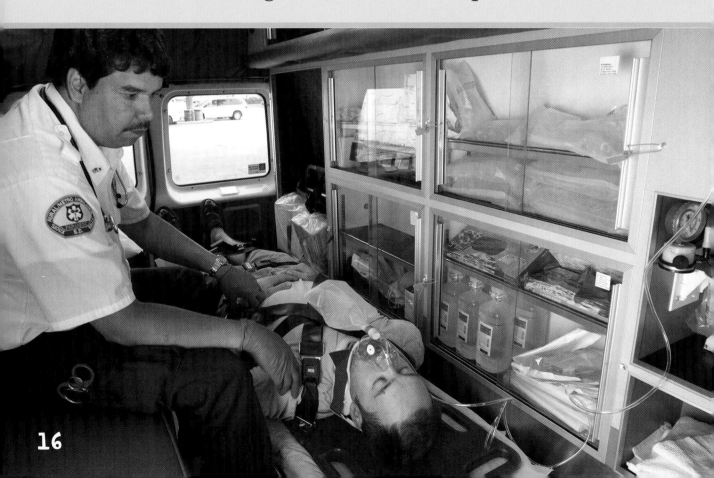

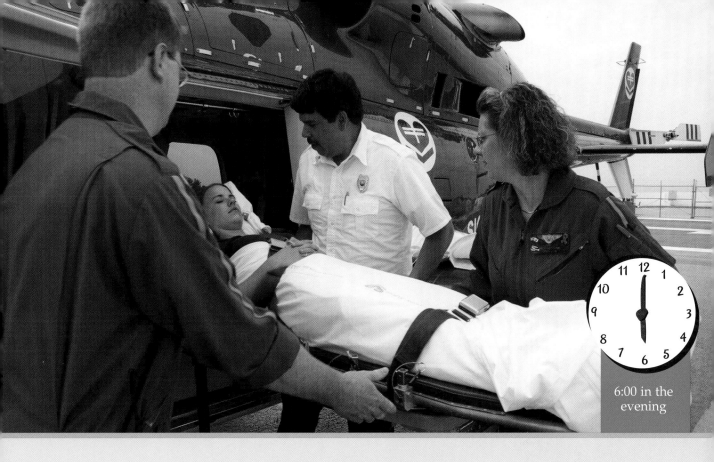

6:00 in the
evening

Sometimes patients need to get to
the hospital quickly. EMTs take patients
to helicopters or airplanes. The patients
are flown to the hospital.

What happens at the end of a shift?

EMTs check the equipment again at the end of their shift. Eugene cleans up the ambulance. He puts more bandages in the drawers. Eugene knows EMTs must always be ready.

Amazing But True!

Bellevue in New York City was the first hospital to use an ambulance service. It started using horses and buggies to carry patients in 1869.

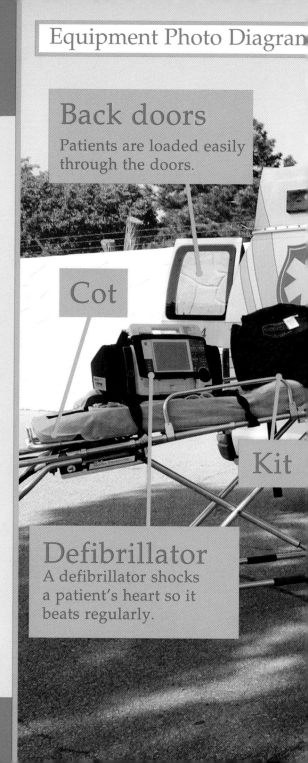

Back doors
Patients are loaded easily through the doors.

Cot

Kit

Defibrillator
A defibrillator shocks a patient's heart so it beats regularly.

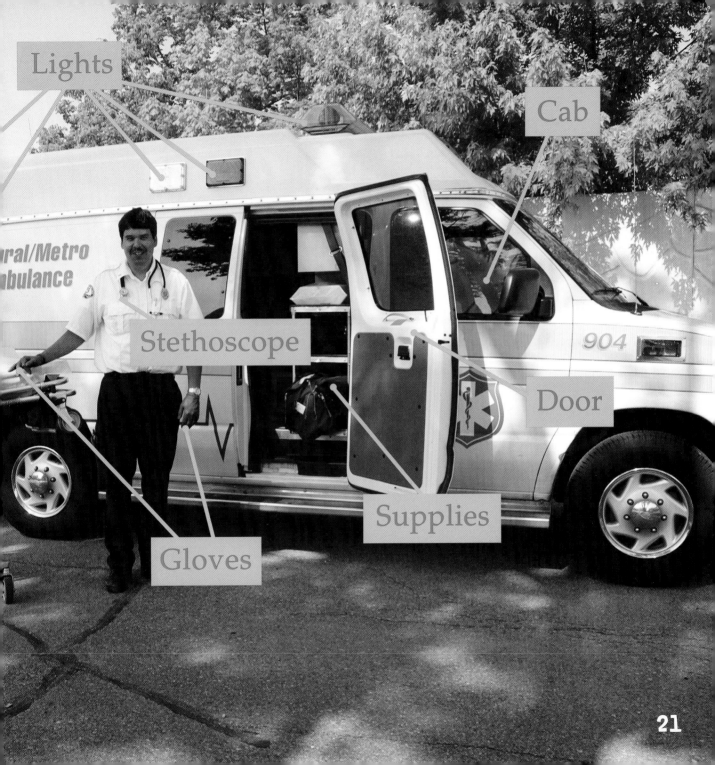

Lights

Cab

Stethoscope

Door

Gloves

Supplies

ral/Metro
mbulance

904

Glossary

ambulance (AM-byuh-luhnss)—a vehicle that takes sick or hurt people to a hospital

chart (CHART)—facts kept about a patient's health

data (DAY-tuh)—information or facts

dispatcher (diss-PACH-ur)—a person who answers 911 calls and assigns rescue workers

emergency (e-MUR-juhn-see)—a sudden or dangerous event

germs (JURMS)—small living things that cause diseases

pulse (PUHLSS)—the steady beat of the heart

shift (SHIFT)—a set amount of time to work

technician (tek-NISH-uhn)—someone who can work with equipment and tools

Read More

Gordon, Sharon. *What's Inside an Ambulance?* What's Inside?
New York: Benchmark Books, 2003.

Mattern, Joanne. *Emergency Medical Technicians.* Working
Together. New York: PowerKids Press, 2002.

Internet Sites

FactHound offers a safe, fun way to find Internet sites related
to this book. All of the sites on FactHound have been
researched by our staff.

Here's how:
1. Visit *www.facthound.com*
2. Type in this special code **073682507X** for
   age-appropriate sites. Or enter a search
   word related to this book for a more
   general search.
3. Click on the Fetch It button.

FactHound will fetch the best sites for you!

Index